Discover The Secret of How to get Joy for your Life and Work

Transforming Your Career and Your Life

John J Love

Copyright © John J Love 2023
All Rights Reserved

Table of contents

Chapter One 2
The Importance of Finding Joy for Your life and Work 2
Chapter Two 2
Identifying Your Passions and Purpose 2
Chapter Three 2
Setting Goals and Creating a Positive Mindset 2
Chapter Four 2
Building Positive Relationships at Work 2
Chapter Five 2
Creating a Positive Work Environment 2
Chapter Six 2
Balancing Your Work and Personal Life 2

Chapter Seven 2
Developing Resilience and Coping with Stress 2
Chapter Eight 2
Fostering Personal and Professional Growth 2
Chapter Nine 2
Finding Meaning and Fulfillment in Your Career 2
Chapter Conclusion 2
Embracing Joy for Your Work Life 2
Introduction 1

Introduction

Welcome To The Transforming of your Career And your Life.
Do you dread going to work every day? Do you feel unfulfilled and uninspired by your job? If so, you're not alone. Many people struggle to find joy and satisfaction in their careers.

But it doesn't have to be this way.

In "The Joy for your life and Work," we will explore Transforming your Career And your Life.

From learning how to set goals and create a positive work environment, to discovering your passions and finding balance, this book will provide you with the tools you need to transform your work life into a source of joy and happiness.

Whether you're just starting in your career or looking to make a change, "The Joy of Work" will show you how to turn your job into a fulfilling and meaningful part of your life. So let's get started on the path to a more joyful career.

Are you tired of feeling burnt out and unfulfilled at work? Do you long for more happiness and satisfaction in your career? If so, "Working Happy" is here to help

In this book, we will explore practical and easy-to-implement transforming your career and your life work. From setting boundaries and finding work-life balance to building positive relationships and developing a growth mindset, this book will provide you with the tools you need to turn your work into a source of happiness and fulfillment.

"Working Happy" is for anyone who wants to find more joy and meaning in their career. Whether you're an entrepreneur, a corporate employee, or anything in between, this book will give you the tools you need to create a happier and more fulfilling work life. So let's get started on the path to a happier career today!

Are you a workaholic who sacrifices your happiness for the sake of your career? Do you struggle to find a balance between your work and your personal life? If so, "The Happy Workaholic" is here to help.

In this book, we will explore how to find joy and fulfillment in your career while also maintaining balance and taking care of yourself. From learning how to set boundaries and prioritize self-care, to finding meaning and purpose in your work, this book will provide you with the tools you need to transform your relationship with your career.

"The Happy Workaholic" is for anyone who wants to find happiness and fulfillment in their career without sacrificing their well-being. If you're ready to learn how to be a successful and happy workaholic, this book is for you.

"The secret of how to get Joy for your life and Workplace.
Transforming Your Career and Your Life"

Do you feel like you're just going through the motions at work? Do you struggle to find joy and fulfillment in your career? If so, "Finding Joy for your life and Workplace" is here to help.

In this book, we will explore practical strategies for finding joy and meaning in your career. From developing a growth mindset and setting goals to building positive relationships and creating a positive work environment, this book will provide you with the tools you need to turn your work into a source of happiness and fulfillment.

"Finding Joy for your life and Workplace" is for anyone who wants to find more joy and satisfaction in their career. Whether you're just starting in your career or looking to make a change, this book will give you the tools you need to create a more fulfilling and meaningful work life.

Chapter One

The Importance of Finding Joy for Your life and Work

The idea of finding joy in your life and work may seem like a foreign concept to some. After all, many people see work as a necessary evil - a means to an end, rather than a source of fulfillment and happiness. However, research has shown that finding joy and meaning in your career can have numerous benefits, both personally and professionally.

On a personal level, finding joy in your life and work can improve your overall well-being and quality of life. It can increase your sense of purpose and meaning, reduce stress and burnout, and contribute to overall happiness and satisfaction.

Professionally, finding joy in your life and your work can lead to increased productivity, creativity, and job satisfaction. It can also improve your relationships with colleagues and contribute to a positive work culture.

Given the numerous benefits of finding joy in your life and your work, it's important to make it a priority. In this book, we will explore transforming your career and your life.

From learning how to set goals and create a positive work environment, to discovering your passions and finding balance, this book will provide you with the tools you need to transform your work life into a source of joy and happiness.

So, let's get started on the journey toward a happier and more fulfilling career!

Chapter Two

Identifying Your Passions and Purpose

Before you can start finding joy in your work, it's important to first identify your passions and purpose. This will help you discover what truly brings you happiness and fulfillment, and guide you toward a career that aligns with your values and interests.

In this chapter, we will explore techniques for identifying your passions and purpose, including:

Reflecting on your values: Take some time to think about what's most important to you in life. What values drive you and give your life meaning? Consider how these values might align with your career choices.

Assessing your interests: Think about what you enjoy doing in your free time. What activities bring you joy and satisfaction? How might these interests translate into a fulfilling career?

Exploring your strengths: Consider what you're naturally good at and enjoy doing. How might these strengths be applied in a career setting?

Seeking guidance: Don't be afraid to seek guidance from others, such as a career counselor or mentor, to help you identify your passions and purpose.

By identifying your passions and purpose, you'll be better equipped to find a career that brings you joy and fulfillment. In the next chapter, we'll delve into how to set goals and create a positive mindset to help you achieve your career aspirations.

Chapter Three

Setting Goals and Creating a Positive Mindset

Once you've identified your passions and purpose, it's important to set goals and cultivate a positive mindset to help you achieve your career aspirations.

In this chapter, we will explore techniques for setting goals and creating a positive mindset, including:

Setting SMART goals: Use the SMART criteria (specific, measurable, achievable, relevant, and time-bound) to set clear and achievable goals for your career.

Creating a growth mindset: Adopt a growth mindset, which is the belief that your abilities and intelligence can be developed through effort and learning. This mindset will help you embrace challenges and setbacks as opportunities for growth and learning.

Visualizing success: Use visualization techniques to help you see and focus on your goals. This can help increase your motivation and confidence as you work towards achieving your career aspirations.

Practicing gratitude: Cultivate an attitude of gratitude by regularly focusing on the things you're thankful for. This can help increase your happiness and satisfaction in your career.

By setting goals and cultivating a positive mindset, you'll be better equipped to achieve your career aspirations and find joy in your work. In the next chapter, we'll delve into how to build positive relationships at work to create a more fulfilling and enjoyable career experience.

Chapter Four

Building Positive Relationships at Work

Having positive relationships with your colleagues can greatly enhance your work experience and contribute to a more enjoyable and fulfilling career. In this chapter, we will explore techniques for building positive relationships at work, including:

Showing appreciation: Show gratitude and appreciation to your colleagues for their contributions and hard work. This can help build trust and respect, and improve overall morale.

Being a good listener: Practice active listening by fully engaging with your colleagues and showing interest in what they have to say. This can help build strong, supportive relationships.

Being a team player: Collaborate with your colleagues and work towards common goals.
This can help build strong bonds and create a more positive work environment.
Being open and approachable: Make an effort to be approachable and open to feedback from your colleagues. This can help build trust and improve communication.
Resolving conflicts: When conflicts do arise, address them constructively and respectfully. This can help improve relationships and create a more positive work environment.
By building positive relationships with your colleagues, you can create a more enjoyable and fulfilling career experience. In the next chapter, we'll delve into how to create a positive work environment to further enhance your work experience.

Chapter Five

Creating a Positive Work Environment

The work environment can have a significant impact on your overall happiness and satisfaction in your career. A positive work environment can foster creativity, productivity, and a sense of belonging, while a negative work environment can lead to stress, burnout, and unhappiness.

In this chapter, we will explore techniques for creating a positive work environment, including:

Cultivating a culture of appreciation: Show gratitude and appreciation to your colleagues and create an atmosphere of positivity.

Encouraging open communication: Foster an open and transparent communication style to help create a sense of trust and belonging.

Providing growth opportunities: Offer opportunities for professional development and growth to help employees feel fulfilled and valued.

Promoting work-life balance: Encourage employees to maintain a healthy work-life balance to prevent burnout and promote overall well-being.

Encouraging teamwork and collaboration: Foster a collaborative and inclusive environment where all employees feel valued and supported.

By creating a positive work environment, you can greatly enhance your work experience and find more joy and fulfillment in your career. In the next chapter, we'll delve into how to find the balance between your work and personal life to further improve your overall well-being.

Chapter Six

Balancing Your Work and Personal Life

Finding a balance between your work and personal life is essential for maintaining your overall well-being and happiness. When we're too focused on work, it can lead to burnout and a lack of fulfillment in other areas of our lives. On the other hand, when we neglect our work responsibilities, it can lead to feelings of guilt and stress.

In this chapter, we will explore techniques for finding the balance between your work and personal life, including:

Setting boundaries: Establish clear boundaries between your work and personal time to prevent work from spilling over into your personal life.

Prioritizing self-care: Make time for self-care activities such as exercise, relaxation, and hobbies to help maintain balance and prevent burnout.

Seeking support: Don't be afraid to seek support from friends, family, or a therapist to help you find balance and manage stress.

Taking breaks: Make sure to take breaks throughout the day to rest and recharge.

By finding the balance between your work and personal life, you can improve your overall well-being and find more joy and fulfillment in your career. In the next chapter, we'll delve into how to develop resilience and cope with stress to further improve your well-being.

Chapter Seven

Developing Resilience and Coping with Stress

Dealing with stress and setbacks is a natural part of any career. It's important to develop resilience and coping mechanisms to help you navigate these challenges and maintain your well-being.

In this chapter, we will explore techniques for developing resilience and coping with stress, including:

Practice mindfulness: Mindfulness practices such as meditation and deep breathing can help you stay present and manage stress.

Exercise and eat well: Taking care of your physical health through exercise and a healthy diet can help improve your resilience and coping skills.

Seek social support: Surround yourself with supportive people who can help you navigate stress and setbacks.

Practice gratitude: Cultivating an attitude of gratitude can help you focus on the positive and find meaning in difficult situations.

Take breaks: Make sure to take breaks and prioritize self-care to prevent burnout and maintain your well-being.

By developing resilience and effective coping skills, you can better navigate the challenges and stress of your career and find more joy and fulfillment in your work. In the next chapter, we'll delve into how to foster personal and professional growth to continue improving and finding meaning in your career.

Chapter Eight

Fostering Personal and Professional Growth

Personal and professional growth is essential for finding fulfillment and happiness in your career. By constantly learning and improving, you can stay engaged and motivated in your work.

In this chapter, we will explore techniques for fostering personal and professional growth, including:

Seek new challenges: Look for opportunities to challenge yourself and learn new skills in your career.

Embrace learning opportunities: Take advantage of training and development opportunities to continue learning and improving.

Find a mentor: Seek guidance from a mentor who can help you navigate your career and identify areas for growth.

Network and seek new opportunities: Expand your professional network and look for new opportunities to grow and advance in your career.

Reflect and set goals: Regularly reflect on your progress and set new goals to continue growing and improving in your career.

By fostering personal and professional growth, you can stay engaged and motivated in your work and find more joy and fulfillment in your career. In the next chapter, we'll delve into how to find meaning and fulfillment in your career to further enhance your work experience.

Chapter Nine

Finding Meaning and Fulfillment in Your Career

Finding meaning and fulfillment in your career is the ultimate goal for many people. It's the feeling that what you do matters and makes a difference in the world.

In this chapter, we will explore techniques for finding meaning and fulfillment in your career, including:

Aligning your career with your values and passions: Choose a career that aligns with your values and passions to help you find meaning and fulfillment.

Making a positive impact: Look for opportunities to make a positive impact in your work, whether it be through helping others or contributing to a cause you believe in.

Finding purpose: Reflect on your strengths and skills and consider how you can use them to make a difference in the world.

Seeking work-life balance: Maintain a healthy work-life balance to help you find meaning and fulfillment in both your personal and professional life.

By finding meaning and fulfillment in your career, you can create a more enjoyable and fulfilling work experience. In the next chapter, we'll delve into how to embrace joy in your work life to further enhance your happiness and satisfaction in your career.

Chapter Conclusion

Embracing Joy for Your Work Life

In this book, we've explored practical strategies for finding joy and fulfillment in your career. From identifying your passions and purpose to setting goals and creating a positive work environment, we've covered a range of techniques to help you transform your work life into a source of happiness and fulfillment.

Remember, finding joy in your work isn't something that happens overnight. It requires effort and commitment to make positive changes in your career. But the rewards of a more fulfilling and enjoyable work life are worth it.

So take the first step towards a more joyful career by implementing the strategies outlined in this book. And most importantly, don't forget to enjoy the journey.

www.ingramcontent.com/pod-product-compliance
Lightning Source LLC
Chambersburg PA
CBHW050329220526
45465CB00005B/2197